City Fish, Country Fish

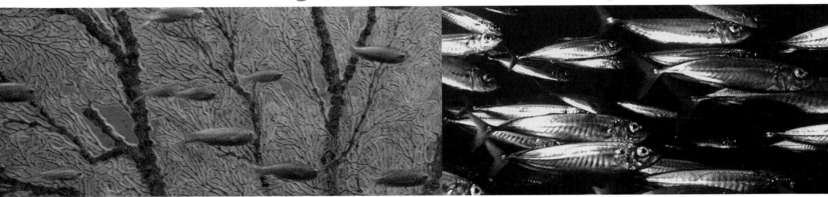

Mary M. Cerullo
Photographs by Jeffrey L. Rotman

TILBURY HOUSE, PUBLISHERS

Gardiner, Maine

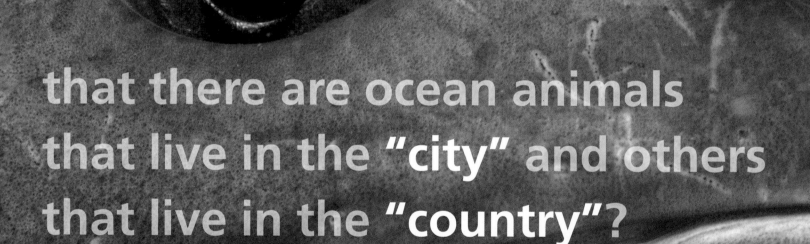

Would you be surprised to learn that there are ocean animals that live in the **"city"** and others that live in the **"country"**?

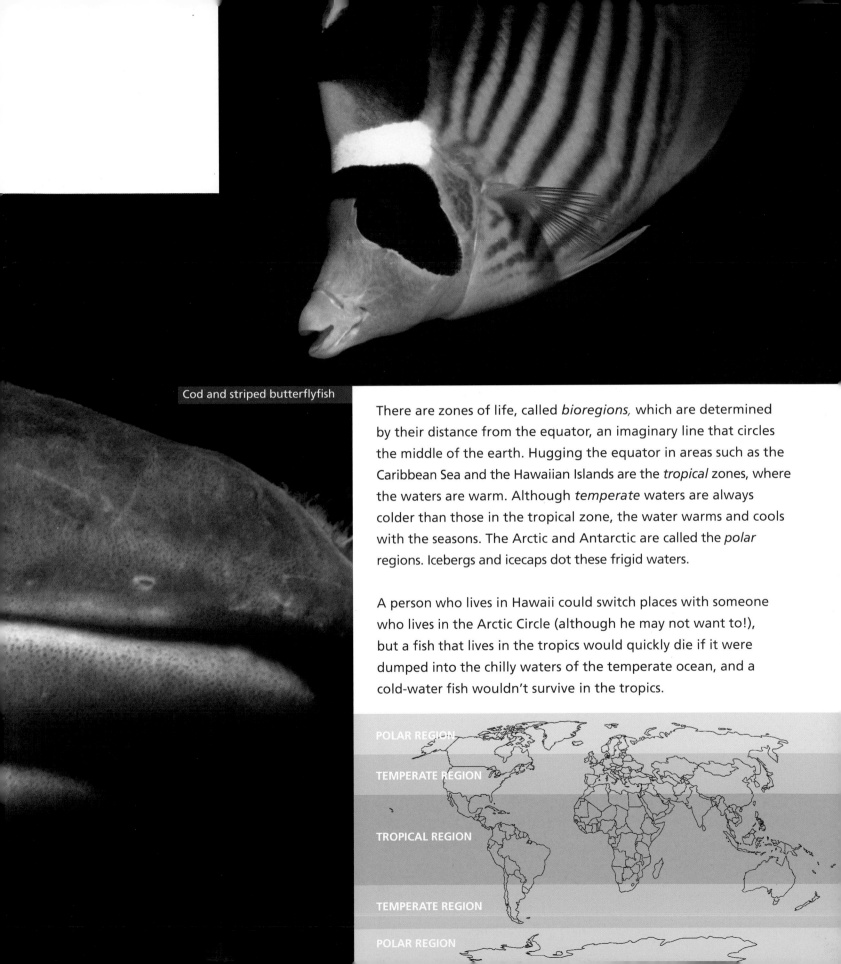

Cod and striped butterflyfish

There are zones of life, called *bioregions,* which are determined by their distance from the equator, an imaginary line that circles the middle of the earth. Hugging the equator in areas such as the Caribbean Sea and the Hawaiian Islands are the *tropical* zones, where the waters are warm. Although *temperate* waters are always colder than those in the tropical zone, the water warms and cools with the seasons. The Arctic and Antarctic are called the *polar* regions. Icebergs and icecaps dot these frigid waters.

A person who lives in Hawaii could switch places with someone who lives in the Arctic Circle (although he may not want to!), but a fish that lives in the tropics would quickly die if it were dumped into the chilly waters of the temperate ocean, and a cold-water fish wouldn't survive in the tropics.

POLAR REGION

TEMPERATE REGION

TROPICAL REGION

TEMPERATE REGION

POLAR REGION

TROPICAL FISHES:
MANY DIFFERENT KINDS, FEW INDIVIDUALS
(DIVERSITY RULES!)

Royal angelfish   Masked butterflyfish

city fish

City fish are tropical fishes that swim in water as warm as a swimming pool. Their home on the coral reef could be called a city under the sea because, like a city on land, a coral reef is busy, crowded, and colorful. A single Caribbean coral reef may be home to more than a thousand different kinds of plants and animals.

A city fish must have "street smarts" to survive. Day or night, it has to defend itself from other fish that would snatch its food, its mate, its hiding place—or the fish itself.

Dusky butterflyfish

A cod lives in the temperate ocean

country fish

COLD-WATER FISHES: MANY INDIVIDUALS, FEWER DIFFERENCES

Country fish swim in cool waters, far from the equator and tropical waters.

Cold-water country fishes such as cod live close to the earth (the ocean floor, actually).

There are not nearly as many different kinds of fishes here as there are in tropical seas— and many of them look pretty much the same. That is not surprising because several belong to the same family. The cod is the largest member of a family that includes pollock, haddock, and hake.

Many cold-water fish travel in giant groups called *schools*. Although this protects them from fish predators, their schooling makes it possible—and profitable—for fishermen to capture thousands of fish at a time.

the colors of the

This tiny coral polyp is the foundation of the largest cities on earth: coral reefs.

Diver and sea raven

oceans

GREEN SOUP: THE COLD OCEANS

Cold waters are a giant food factory. Minerals washed into the ocean from the land mix with nutritious morsels stirred up from the ocean floor. They become fertilizers for microscopic floating plants. These *phytoplankton* bloom in huge numbers and are eaten by tiny animals called *zooplankton*. Together, phytoplankton and zooplankton support a huge food web, which includes cod, other fishes, and the animals that eat those fishes.

The phytoplankton near the ocean's surface absorb some of the sun's light, making the water appear green. For much of the year, the water is murky—or, as some would say, "as thick as pea soup." The fishes that live here think of this plankton soup as "dinner."

BLUE SEAS: THE TROPICAL OCEANS

The first thing you notice about the tropical ocean is its color: a bright, inviting turquoise. Dive in and you can see deep into the water— below, above, and all around. A city fish may feel as if it can see forever, but even so, it rarely strays far from its home on the coral reef.

Like an oasis in the desert, a coral reef provides the only food and shelter for miles around. There are few food particles suspended in the clear water. Any animal that ventures far from the reef is easily spotted by roaming predators.

Giant kelp forest

No Trespassing!
The warning colors on a spotfin lionfish should discourage any attackers.

ELECTRIC COLORS

It's not just the color of the water in the tropics that captures your attention. Coral reef fishes brighten the reef with reds, yellows, and blues, and with stripes, spots, and splotches.

Like billboards in the city, eye-catching colors can advertise a message of welcome or of warning. A splash of color can help an angelfish attract a mate, while the deadly lionfish uses its stripes to warn intruders that it's not wise to tangle with the sharp, venomous spines that ripple along its back.

It's not easy to find the right balance between being noticed by your friends and becoming a target for your enemies. To solve that problem, a coral reef fish may flash a brilliant color to draw the attention of a female. After a brief encounter, he may quickly change back to a less flashy look. At dusk, the bright colors of some coral reef fishes fade to dark "pajama stripes" as they head off to bed.

Royal angelfish

# of fishes

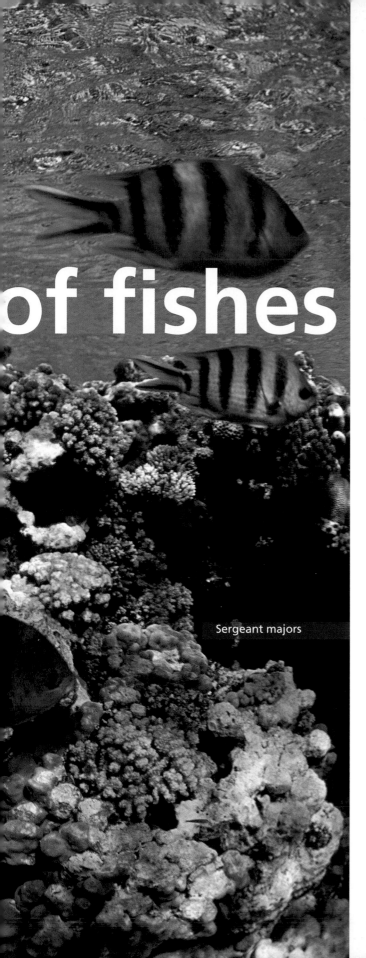

Sergeant majors

Sea raven

EARTH TONES

While city fish often use vivid color to stand out against the coral reef, country fish use camouflage, like hunters in the forest, to hide in plain sight. The colors of country fish are mostly earth tones—tan, brown, and black—that mimic the colors of the seaweeds and rocks on the ocean floor. Those that travel in schools near the ocean's surface tend to have silvery scales that reflect back the light, like waves on water.

Many kinds of fishes can change their skin color to blend in with their surroundings, but the flounder does it best. As it swims across the ocean floor, you can actually watch its color change as it crosses from light sand to dark gravel.

Tiny sacs of pigment called *chromatophores* stretch or shrink to make the flounder change color.

living
space

HIGH-RISE CONDOS

A coral reef occupies a relatively small slice of ocean real estate. It's bounded on one side by land, usually an island or the eastern coast of a continent. On the other side, the ocean may drop off sharply into a deep abyss. Since space is tight, there is a lot of competition for hiding places. Even the smallest fishes, with dainty names like angelfish, damselfish, and butterfly-fish, are ready to rumble to protect their precious pieces of reef.

Like residents in a high-rise apartment, fishes live at well-defined levels on the coral reef. After a hard day of foraging for food, they return to the same retreats night after night.

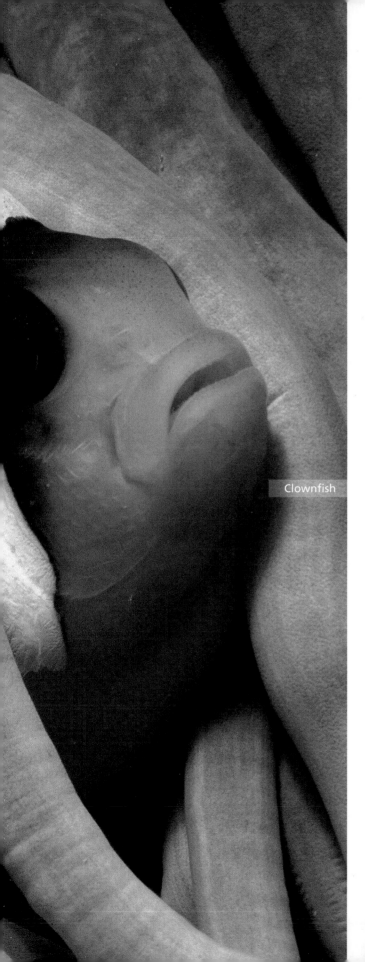
Clownfish

ROOM TO ROAM

There are advantages to not being tied to one place. If an area becomes polluted, country fish may be able to move elsewhere until conditions improve. Many times, though, pollution such as sewage or an oil spill can damage a habitat so much that the animals can no longer live there.

Many country fish spend their lives roaming the ocean just a few feet above the sea floor. They are even called *groundfish* by the fishermen who drag their nets along the ocean bottom to harvest them.

Cod have a special chin whisker called a *barbel* for feeling and tasting clams, crabs, and other seafood that lives on the ocean floor.

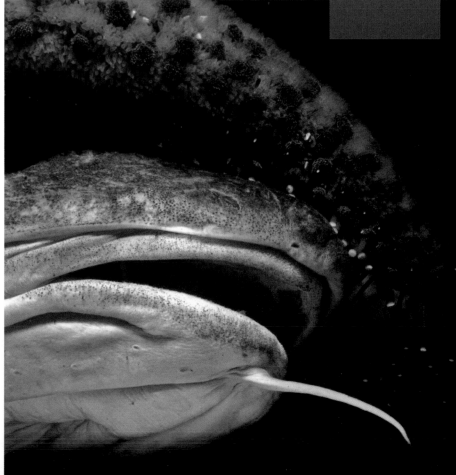

Some slinky reef residents, such as moray eels, slither into tunnels inside the reef.

the shape

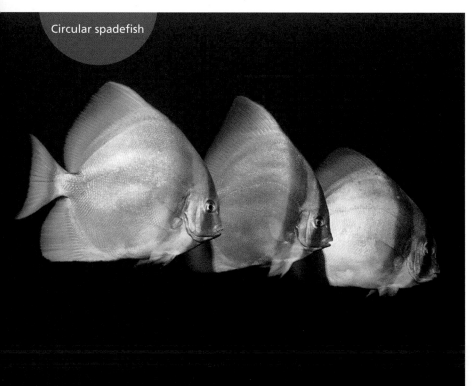

Circular spadefish

FLAT AND COMPACT

Many city fish are not built for long-distance travel because they rarely venture far from the security of their undersea refuge. Instead, coral reef fishes are designed for quick escape. Many are flattened from side to side like DVDs. When a scary shadow passes overhead, they dive into hiding places within the coral branches. A large tail and short side fins help them brake and swerve fast, like tiny sports cars.

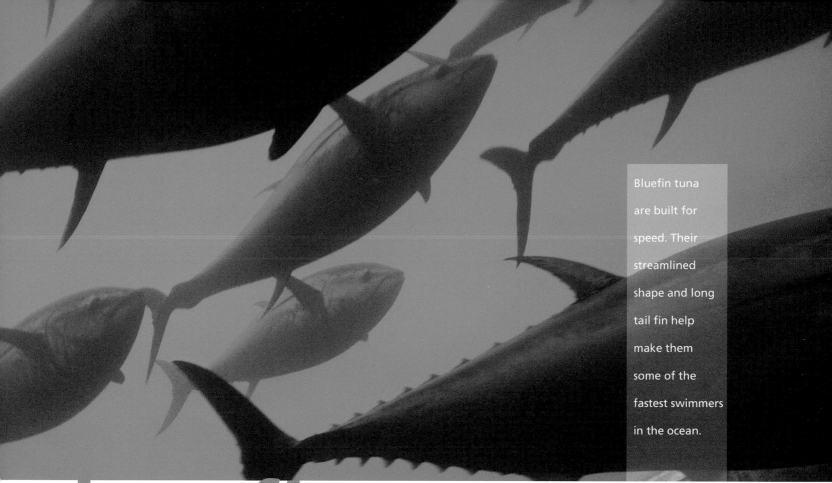

Bluefin tuna are built for speed. Their streamlined shape and long tail fin help make them some of the fastest swimmers in the ocean.

that fits

SOLID AND STURDY

Most country fish are robust and hardy, built for swimming long distances. It's no coincidence that we humans have designed our underwater vehicles to resemble their streamlined "submarine" shape.

Other country fish are adapted to fit flat against the ocean floor. A skate, the cold-water relative of a stingray, buries itself in sand up to its eyeballs. It breathes through holes in the top of its head called *spiracles.* If it tried to breathe by taking water in through its mouth, located underneath, it would gulp in a mouthful of sand instead.

Skate

working together

SYMBIOSIS

Here on the reef, unexpected alliances between different creatures help to keep the reef healthy. When a partnership helps one or both creatures, it is called *symbiosis*, which means "living together." For example, a cleaner fish removes parasites that irritate the skin, mouth, and gills of larger fishes. A customer fish stays still to allow the cleaner to scour its teeth like a diminutive dentist. What do cleaner fish get by performing this good deed? A hearty meal.

A moray eel will allow a cleaner fish to swim right inside its mouth to clean food particles off its teeth.

The clownfish finds a hiding place inside its symbiotic partner, a sea anemone. In exchange, it lures other fishes into its host's stinging tentacles.

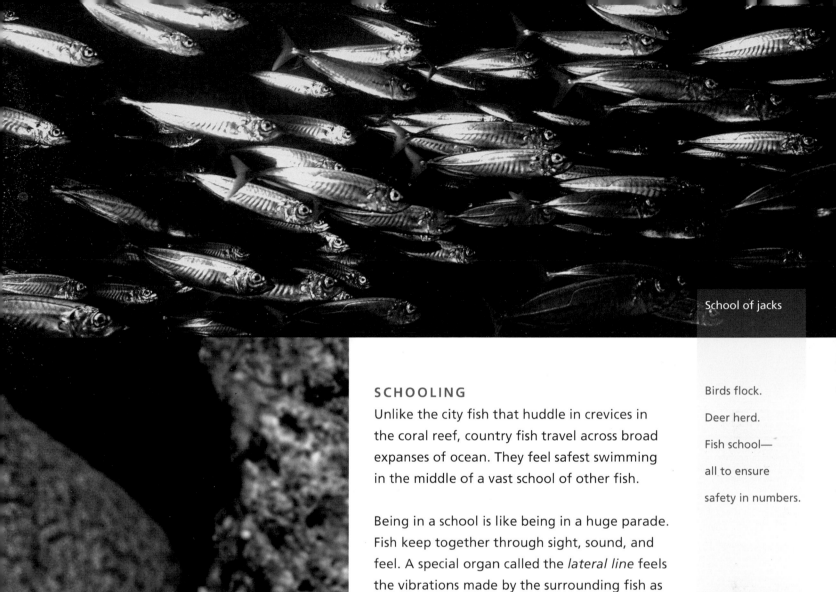

School of jacks

SCHOOLING

Unlike the city fish that huddle in crevices in the coral reef, country fish travel across broad expanses of ocean. They feel safest swimming in the middle of a vast school of other fish.

Being in a school is like being in a huge parade. Fish keep together through sight, sound, and feel. A special organ called the *lateral line* feels the vibrations made by the surrounding fish as they move through the water.

A school of fish has many eyes and other senses to detect predators and to locate prey. A predator usually targets one fish within the school. If you were a fish in the middle of a school, chances are that the predator would not choose *you.*

Birds flock.

Deer herd.

Fish school—

all to ensure

safety in numbers.

secrets of

The parrotfish's teeth have fused together to make a "beak" that can gnaw away at the hard coral to get to the tiny plants that live inside.

SPECIALIZATIONS HELP SOME STAND OUT FROM THE CROWD

All animals have two basic requirements for survival: finding food and avoiding becoming someone else's food. Like in cities on land, there are many kinds of specialists doing business on the reef that help make those tasks easier.

Some coral reef fishes have specialized mouths for getting at just the right meal. The long-nosed butterflyfish has a snout that can poke into narrow openings in the reef to grab tiny shrimp and worms.

Other fishes have hidden weapons to surprise would-be predators. The surgeonfish has spines as sharp as a surgeon's knife concealed on either side of its tail. These spines spring open the instant the fish senses danger.

Longnose butterflyfish

Orange-spine unicornfish

SELF-RELIANT FISHES

Cold-water fishes rely less on specializations and more on strength and stamina. Generally, they use their swimming ability to escape predators and to find food and mates. Many cold-water fishes grow quite large and swim thousands of miles. Migrating fishes need energy and endurance—and the ability to find their way back again.

Unlike some coral reef fishes that subsist on a very particular diet, many country fish eat whatever comes their way. With a mouth the size of a garbage can lid, the goosefish eats almost anything it can fit into its mouth. It lures flounder, lobsters, and sea snails with a wriggling "worm" that is actually a piece of its own skin. Goosefish sometimes grab ducks or gulls resting on the ocean surface. (So far, it's never been proven that goosefish have eaten geese!)

survival

Goosefish

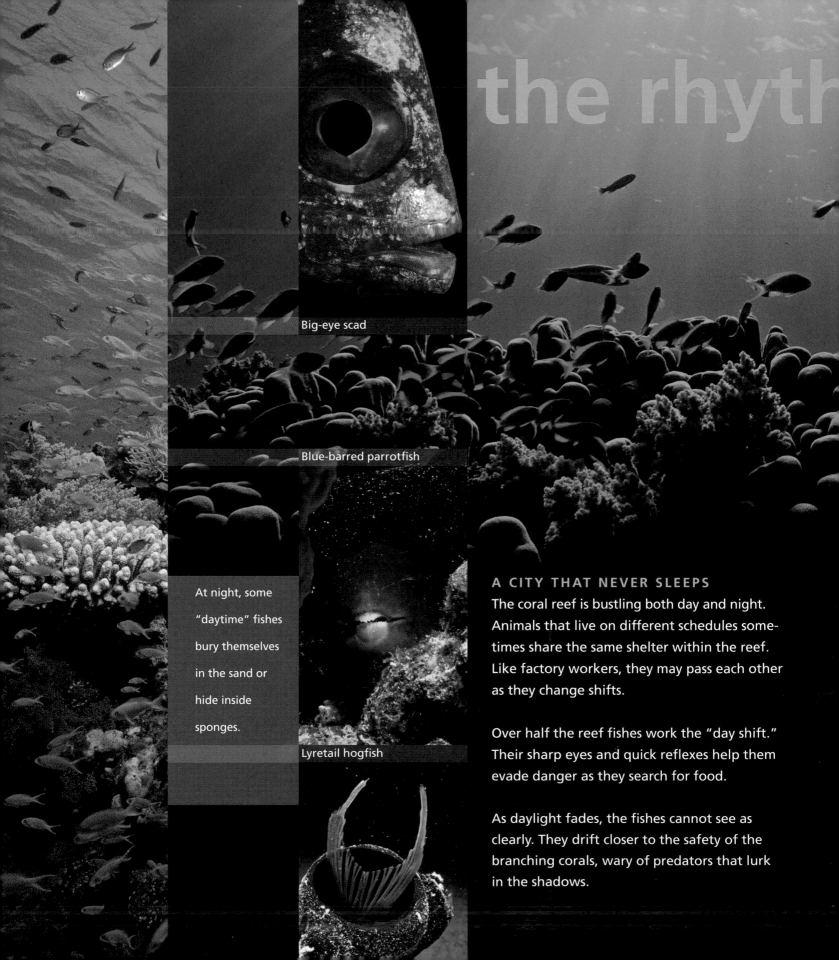

Big-eye scad

Blue-barred parrotfish

At night, some "daytime" fishes bury themselves in the sand or hide inside sponges.

Lyretail hogfish

A CITY THAT NEVER SLEEPS

The coral reef is bustling both day and night. Animals that live on different schedules sometimes share the same shelter within the reef. Like factory workers, they may pass each other as they change shifts.

Over half the reef fishes work the "day shift." Their sharp eyes and quick reflexes help them evade danger as they search for food.

As daylight fades, the fishes cannot see as clearly. They drift closer to the safety of the branching corals, wary of predators that lurk in the shadows.

Cod

While other creatures patrol the night reef, a parrotfish rests in its sleeping bag, sealed inside a mucous bubble that keeps its scent hidden from hungry moray eels.

At night, a different community appears. Fishes like the big-eye scad can detect movement in the darkness.

A YEAR IN THE LIFE

The rhythm of life is slower in cold waters. Changes here happen over 365 days instead of 24 hours. Rather like classes of students are known by the year in which they will graduate from high school, fishes such as cod and haddock are known by their *year class,* the year they were born. Fishermen eagerly wait for a large year class to grow big enough to be harvested.

The cycle of life is tied to the changing seasons. In spring, longer days with more sunlight set the stage for rebirth. The first crop of phytoplankton blooms in early spring, followed by another bloom in late summer. As if on cue, tiny animals such as baby crabs, fishes, and lobsters hatch to take advantage of the sudden surge in food supply.

Cunners

Whitetip reef shark

Great white shark

cruising

RAIDERS OF THE REEF

At dawn and dusk on the coral reef, unwelcome guests show up like uninvited relatives at a family reunion. Sharks appear on the reef at daybreak and nightfall. These distant cousins of the reef residents wait in the shadows to attack weary fishes returning from feeding.

Many kinds of sharks roam tropical waters, but whitetip reef sharks can often be seen hanging around the same coral reef year after year.

These sharks may hunt in packs of a hundred or more. Some chase small fish into tunnels inside the reef while others wait on the other side and grab the frightened fish as they flee through another exit

The great white shark is uniquely suited for patrolling the cool waters of the world's oceans. Most fishes are cold-blooded, which means their body temperature takes on the temperature of the surrounding water. But great white sharks are warm-blooded, making them able to respond faster. A heat exchange system warms up their muscles and increases their speed and reaction time, similar to the way

cousins

Predators like this whitetip reef shark eating a surgeonfish help keep ocean ecosystems healthy by controlling populations of resident fish.

Sea lions

a runner warms up before a race. Raising their stomach temperature also helps great whites digest their food faster.

The great white shark prefers fatty food like seals, sea lions, and whales, which often are found in cooler waters. This should make us feel better. Compared to these plump prey, why would a great white shark seek out a bony human?

we are all the same

Sapphire gurnard

but different

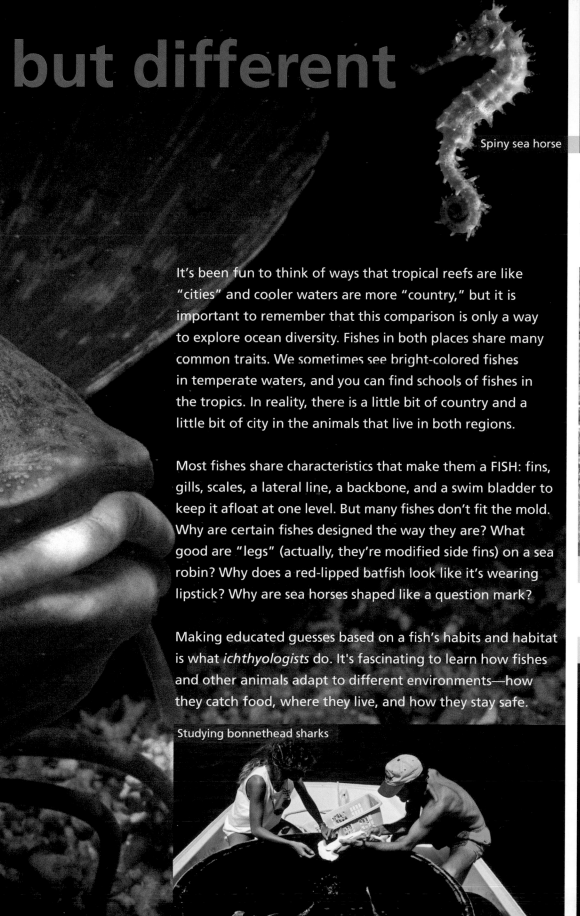

Spiny sea horse

Swordfish

Some fish, such as swordfish and tuna, can sprint through the water at speeds approaching 80 kilometers an hour (50 mph).

It's been fun to think of ways that tropical reefs are like "cities" and cooler waters are more "country," but it is important to remember that this comparison is only a way to explore ocean diversity. Fishes in both places share many common traits. We sometimes see bright-colored fishes in temperate waters, and you can find schools of fishes in the tropics. In reality, there is a little bit of country and a little bit of city in the animals that live in both regions.

Most fishes share characteristics that make them a FISH: fins, gills, scales, a lateral line, a backbone, and a swim bladder to keep it afloat at one level. But many fishes don't fit the mold. Why are certain fishes designed the way they are? What good are "legs" (actually, they're modified side fins) on a sea robin? Why does a red-lipped batfish look like it's wearing lipstick? Why are sea horses shaped like a question mark?

Making educated guesses based on a fish's habits and habitat is what *ichthyologists* do. It's fascinating to learn how fishes and other animals adapt to different environments—how they catch food, where they live, and how they stay safe.

Red-lipped batfish

Studying bonnethead sharks

Pufferfish

Stingrays

When a scuba diver enters the ocean, he or she takes on the characteristics of a fish. Rubber flippers act like fishy fins to help in swimming. A face mask, like a fish's glassy eyes, helps a person see clearly underwater. An air tank is our answer to gills. A weight belt and a buoyancy compensator vest allow a human to stay in one place, the way a swim bladder works for a fish.

DIVING WHERE IT'S CROWDED AND COLORFUL

Giant Napoleon wrasse

When you dive into a coral sea, chances are the reef residents will scatter as you splash into their neighborhood. Once they get used to you, they may reappear, allowing you to study their fantastic colors and complex social scene— at least from a distance.

Underwater photographer Jeff Rotman says, "If you happen to be diving in the tropics on a perfect day, you can see for more than 200 feet. What you can't see are the invisible boundaries that fishes set. It might be 3 feet or it might be 80 feet, but they will not allow you to cross that boundary."

can become fish

Photographer
Jeff Rotman's son,
Matthew, age 9,
left, encounters
a giant 14-pound
lobster.

WHERE DIVING IS FULL OF SURPRISES

Cold-water diving is also an adventure in many ways. You must wear a wetsuit to stay warm. Sometimes you get so turned around in the murky water that you can't even tell which way is up.

Says Jeff, "I feel a sense of mystery whenever I'm diving in cold waters. I usually can't see more than 10 feet around me, so it's no wonder I never see multitudes of fishes. They sense my presence before I ever see them and stay clear of me. Because it is so cold and difficult to work in cold-water habitats, fewer divers have explored them, so there is much that remains to be discovered there."

For now, humans can only be visitors to the ocean. Whether you visit the "city" or the "country," remember that you are a guest and be respectful of the residents.

Diver with

cunners

the ocean is

How many fishes are in the ocean? Estimates range from 14,000 to 28,000 species, but those are just guesses. Chances are there are many more fishes out there that we don't even know about yet.

Tropical reef fishes live in clear, warm waters that show off their bright colors and special adaptations. Cold-water fishes swim through a feast of plankton-rich waters. Their differences help them survive in their part of the ocean.

Those differences make the ocean a better place to live. That huge variety—what scientists call "diversity"—is important for maintaining the health of the oceans.

School of barracuda

Sargeant majors

Purple anthias

a great place to live

A healthy ocean isn't just important to fishes; a healthy ocean is important to us people. Not only does the ocean provide half the oxygen we breathe, it affects our weather, challenges our skills, and nurtures our spirits.

Fishes face dangers that they cannot control—but we can. Fishes can't protect their communities from pollution, overfishing, and warming temperatures. For that, they must rely on the kindness of strangers—people who work to protect the world's oceans.

After all, city or country, fishes or people, above or below the waves—it's all one world.

GLOSSARY

abyss a deep canyon in the ocean with straight walls

barbel a whiskerlike projection on the lower jaw of certain fishes such as catfish and cod

bioregion an area with the required range of temperatures and other environmental conditions that certain animals and plants need to survive

buoyancy compensator vest worn by a diver to keep afloat at a desired level in the ocean

camouflage any kind of coloring that helps an animal blend in with its surroundings

chromatophore a tiny sac of pigment that stretches or shrinks to make an animal change color

cold-blooded a condition in an animal, such as a fish or a reptile, in which its body temperature changes with the temperature of the surrounding environment

diversity variety in nature; many different kinds of plants, animals, and habitats help an ecosystem resist or recover quickly from diseases, pollution, and other disturbances

ecosystem how living things and their environment function as a unit

equator an imaginary line around the middle of the earth that separates the Northern and Southern Hemispheres

food web the complex relationship of who eats whom in a community

groundfish a fish that spends most of its life swimming near the ocean floor

ichthyologist a scientist who studies fish

lateral line a line of sensory organs along the length of a fish that detect vibrations in the water

nutrient a nourishing substance

phytoplankton microscopic plants that drift on the current; literally, "wanderers"

polar relating to, connected with, or located near the North Pole or South Pole

polyp the nonswimming stage of a coral or a sea anemone, shaped like a hollow cup with tentacles surrounding the open end

scuba stands for self-contained underwater breathing apparatus, based on the device developed by Emile Gagnan and Jacques Cousteau, which uses a tank of compressed gas (usually air)

spiracles small openings on either side of a ray's eyes where water is drawn in and then passed over its gills

swim bladder an organ that inflates or deflates with gas to keep a fish at a certain level in the water

symbiosis when two different species live together and at least one benefits

temperate describing an area that is moderate in temperature; although the seasonal changes are apparent, it is not subject to prolonged extremes of hot or cold weather

tropical an area that is warm year-round, typically near or on the equator

warm-blooded having a body temperature that stays the same no matter what the temperature of its surroundings

year class the year in which a group of fish is born, which identifies it for the rest of their lives and is typically used by scientists and fishermen to describe fish available for harvesting

zooplankton small, drifting animals that feed on phytoplankton or other zooplankton; sometimes the baby stage of animals such as fish and crabs

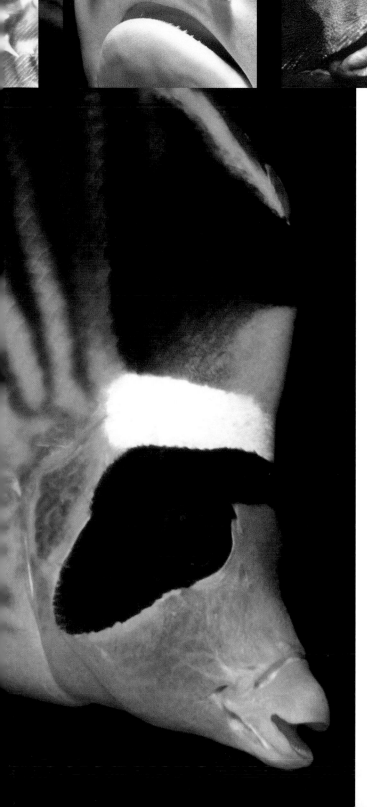

FISH OR FISHES?

Scientists use fish as a plural to describe a number of fish of the same kind, or species; they use fishes when they are talking about several different kinds, such as the variety of fishes one might find on a coral reef.

DIVING DEEPER

The Cod's Tale, Mark Kurlansky
(New York: G.P. Putnam's Sons, 2001)

Swimmy, Leo Lionni
(New York: Pantheon Books, 1963)

Coral Reef: A City That Never Sleeps, Mary M. Cerullo
(New York: Cobblehill, 1996)

The Truth about Great White Sharks, Mary M. Cerullo
(San Francisco: Chronicle, 2000)

The Truth about Dangerous Marine Animals, Mary M. Cerullo
(San Francisco: Chronicle, 2003)

Sea Soup: Phytoplankton, Mary M. Cerullo
(Gardiner, Maine: Tilbury House, 1999)

Sea Soup: Zooplankton, Mary M. Cerullo
(Gardiner, Maine: Tilbury House, 2001)

Surrounded by Sea: Life on a New England Fishing Island,
Gail Gibbons (Boston: Little, Brown, 1991)

TILBURY HOUSE, PUBLISHERS

103 Brunswick Avenue, Gardiner, Maine 04345

800–582–1899 · www.tilburyhouse.com

First hardcover edition: May 1, 2012 · 10 9 8 7 6 5 4 3 2 1

DEDICATIONS

For the one with the sea and the sky in her name: Taylor Marina Cerullo —MMC

For my favorite dive buddies: Matthew and Thomas Rotman —JLR

ACKNOWLEDGMENTS

Many thanks to Dr. John Annala, Chief Scientific Officer, Gulf of Maine Research Institute, and former Chief Scientist, New Zealand Ministry of Fishes, and to Brian Tarbox, Assistant Professor of Marine Science, Southern Maine Community College, for their assistance in developing the concepts and reviewing the final text. Thanks also to Doreen Kirchner for working her artistic magic with the photographs; Isabelle Delafosse for helping to select the images in this book; and Karen Fisk and Jennifer Bunting for their encouragement. I am also grateful to Jeff Rotman, who with over thirty years' experience diving with fishes, contributed his unique insight to the text of this book. Any errors are the author's alone.

LIBRARY OF CONGRESS CATALOGING-IN-PUBLICATION DATA

Cerullo, Mary M.

City fish, country fish / Mary M. Cerullo ; photographs by Jefffrey L. Rotman. — 1st hardcover ed.

p. cm.

ISBN 978-0-88448-323-6 (hardcover : alk. paper)

1. Coral reef fishes—Juvenile literature. 2. Marine fishes—Cold regions—Juvenile literature. I. Rotman, Jeffrey L., ill II. Title.

QL620.45.C47 2012

597.177'89—dc23

2011026591

Designed by Geraldine Millham, Westport, Massachusetts

Printed and bound by Sung In Printing Ltd., Dang Jung-Dong 242-2, GungPo-si, Kyunggi-do, Korea; February 2012